Another Gospel? Participant's Guide

Another Gospel?

Six Sessions on the Search

for Truth in Response to the Claims

of Progressive Christianity

Alisa Childers

WITH NANCY TAYLOR

TYNDALE
MOMENTUM®

A Tyndale nonfiction imprint

Visit Tyndale online at www.tyndale.com.

Visit Tyndale Momentum online at www.tyndalemomentum.com.

Visit Alisa Childers at alisachilders.com.

TYNDALE, Tyndale's quill logo, *Tyndale Momentum*, and the Tyndale Momentum logo
are registered trademarks of Tyndale House Ministries. Tyndale Momentum is a nonfiction
imprint of Tyndale House Publishers, Carol Stream, Illinois.

Published in association with the literary agency of William K. Jensen Literary Agency,
119 Bampton Court, Eugene, OR 97404.

For information about special discounts for bulk purchases, please contact Tyndale House
Publishers at csresponse@tyndale.com, or call 1-855-277-9400.

Library of Congress Cataloging-in-Publication Data

A catalog record for this book is available from the Library of Congress.

ISBN 978-1-4964-6457-6

Printed in the United States of America

28	27	26	25	24	23	22
7	6	5	4	3	2	1

Contents

A Note from Alisa Childers

You know that feeling when you're scrolling through Facebook and read a blog post that seems off—but you can't quite articulate why? Do you feel confused by what *seems* like a loving and inclusive message coming from progressive Christians? Are you concerned about the progressive movement and looking for a concise resource to help you identify and respond to its claims and practices (plus have a handy guide to give to your less-concerned friends)?

I'm so thrilled you have chosen to come on this journey with me! I once was thrown into a faith crisis that I had absolutely no idea how to navigate. As a lifelong believer in Jesus, I never doubted what I believed until I met a clever skeptic who also happened to be a pastor. More specifically, he was a progressive Christian pastor. Suddenly, I was left with more questions than answers, and my faith was hanging by a thread. *Another Gospel?* is the story of my journey through doubt and deconstruction, and ultimately to a firm and intellectually informed faith.

This participant's guide and the *Another Gospel?* DVD

Experience have been created as companions to my book. Over the course of the next six weeks, you will walk with me via video and utilize this wonderful resource that Nancy Taylor and the team at Tyndale put together and adapted from *Another Gospel?* My prayer is that you will come out on the other side with a stronger faith and a deeper confidence as you minister to those in your life who may be caught up in progressive Christianity.

Introduction

There's a storm coming. At some point you'll be caught in a deluge you didn't see on the horizon. The winds will whip around you, the floodwaters will surge beneath your feet, and you'll cry out in alarm, wondering if anyone hears you or is able to help. I'm not talking about a literal storm, although that might be part of your story. I'm talking about a crisis of faith that makes you doubt everything you thought you knew about God. It may be life circumstances that throw you off-balance, leading you to question what you thought you knew about God. Or perhaps it will be the winds of culture and false doctrine that buffet you, making you realize that your belief system is built on sand and won't be able to withstand the tempest you're in. Whatever the nature of your storm, it may leave you disoriented and confused about core issues of the Christian faith that you thought you had settled.

The truth is, we all have questions and doubts about God and his ways. The storms of life just bring them to the forefront of our minds and make them impossible to ignore.

Thankfully, there are real answers to our existential questions that make logical sense, and God wants to help us discover them.

Sometimes we might think that if we keep on nagging God about our doubts, he will get tired of us. We might think he's more pleased with us if we just keep going through the motions of the Christian life and ignore the questions that pop into our minds. We might think that faith is the opposite of doubt. But nothing could be further from the truth. Jesus promised, "Keep on asking, and you will receive what you ask for. Keep on seeking, and you will find. Keep on knocking, and the door will be opened to you. For everyone who asks, receives. Everyone who seeks, finds. And to everyone who knocks, the door will be opened" (Matthew 7:7-8). God wants us to be persistent in coming to him over and over, and he wants us to search for answers until we find the truth.

Likewise, the apostle James said, "If you need wisdom, ask our generous God, and he will give it to you. He will not rebuke you for asking. But when you ask him, be sure that your faith is in God alone. Do not waver, for a person with divided loyalty is as unsettled as a wave of the sea that is blown and tossed by the wind" (James 1:5-6). God is the source of wisdom, and when we ask him to give it to us, he lavishes it on us. But that second part of James's teaching is important. If we want to be settled and stable through the storms of life, we have to be secure in what we believe. Our faith needs to be in God alone, the Rock of Ages.

That's what the book *Another Gospel?* is all about. Our

churches and neighborhoods are full of people who are asking big questions: Who is the God of the Bible? What about
heaven and hell—are those just metaphors? If they're real,
what does that say about what God is like? Can the Bible
even be trusted? What does an ancient faith have to do with
my life today? These are important questions to consider,
and by answering them with the truth we can build a sure
foundation for our faith.

That's what we all want, in the final analysis. We want
something to cling to when we are facing death and disas-
ter. We want something certain when everything around
us seems to be shifting and unstable. And we want something worth building our lives around. Paul said this type
of structurally sound faith that can withstand life's storms
is the goal of the Christian life: "Then we will no longer be
immature like children. We won't be tossed and blown about
by every wind of new teaching. We will not be influenced
when people try to trick us with lies so clever they sound like
the truth. Instead, we will speak the truth in love, growing in
every way more and more like Christ, who is the head of his
body, the church" (Ephesians 4:14-15).

The problem isn't that we're distressed by the storms that
come into our lives or that we are asking questions about
the faith. After all, even the disciples thought a storm was
going to wipe them out, and many writers of Scripture
asked God questions and sometimes even argued with him!
The problem is that all too often people are looking for
answers in the wrong places, and sometimes for the wrong
reasons.

Looking for Answers in All the Right Places

Where are we going to go with these doubts, questions, and debates? Will we let God answer through the evidence we can observe in nature and in his Word, or will we instead listen to the answers culture is providing? Are we going to wallow in disbelief, or will we bring our honest doubts to God and seek the truth? Are we willing to take the risk of getting to the bedrock issues of faith? And once we get there, will we submit our lives to God? Do we want to have answers to our questions even if it means our lives will be more difficult?

This study guide will lead you on a journey of discovery. We'll look at the big questions people are asking—which may be questions you are asking yourself, or maybe you're encountering them in your church, from a family member, or on social media, or maybe you haven't even thought of them yet. No question is too big or too small, and nothing is off-limits. If we want answers, we have to be willing to ask the questions.

Then we'll point out the so-called answers that progressive Christianity provides. Those answers often satisfy our "itching ears" (2 Timothy 4:3). They appeal to our desire for love and acceptance, and that's why so many are lured in by them. But there are significant problems with the basic structure of reality presented by progressive Christianity, and those logical fallacies need to be pointed out. Their answers are sometimes incomplete and sometimes altogether false, and in the end leave us hopeless and helpless. That's why this book will bring you straight to the source of all wisdom and truth: God himself, and the revelation he has provided in the Bible and in his creation.

This study is designed to be done in community, alongside other travelers who are searching for truth. When we listen to others, we gain perspective on both the questions that need to be asked and the contrasting answers provided by culture and God's Word. To continue the analogy of navigating the storms of life, we can read the map together and help each other find the best place to drop anchor. Best of all, by studying in community we will realize that we're not alone—other people are there to share our struggles along the way and celebrate when we arrive at the destination.

Tips for Participants

One word of advice: As with anything in life, you'll get out of this study what you put in. If you go to each meeting to watch the video and have a discussion with your group, you'll learn a little something. Your time will have been well spent. But you won't have gotten everything out of the experience that you could have. If, on the other hand, you prepare ahead of time by reading the recommended chapters in *Another Gospel?* and then answering the reflection questions after your meeting, you'll gain far more understanding, insight, and tools for the next steps in your faith walk. If this is worth doing, it's worth doing well.

To gain the most from this study you should set aside two or three hours per week to prepare. After each week's meeting, you can either answer the reflection questions and then read the next session's chapters from the book in one sitting, or break it up into two or three blocks of time. Does that sound like a lot? It's not as much as you might think. Just replace one night of mindlessly binge-watching Netflix with some reflection and reading time. Or take two lunch hours per week to read the book instead of scrolling Instagram. Better yet, head to your local coffee shop on a Saturday morning with your book in hand, along with a pen for underlining and writing in the margins. The time you put into this study will pay dividends in your own faith journey as well as your relationships with fellow believers who may ask you questions related to their own faith. For the reading portions, you can even listen to the audiobook, which frees you up to do other things while you learn, like drive to work, clean your house, or work out.

Once you're in the group, come ready to share. Your group will succeed or fail based on how open people are willing to be. Come with your honest questions, come ready to listen with an open mind and heart, and be vulnerable with fellow group members. If you have a question or concern, probably someone else in the group does too. Your listening ear and gracious responses to one another will create an atmosphere where faith can grow and flourish.

But don't overshare. Your group needs to be a safe place for everyone, and that means you need to hold confidences that have been spoken. Don't gossip or slander people. It's enough to share broad strokes of things you've seen or experienced—people don't need to know all your concerns about your wayward child or the church across town your brother-in-law's aunt heard something about. And while we're on the topic of oversharing, remember to leave time and space for the introverts in your midst to speak up.

General good group manners also say that you should arrive on time and attend every week that you possibly can. It's a way of respecting others. When one person is late or missing, the whole group suffers.

How This Study Works

There are six sessions in this study, corresponding with chapters from *Another Gospel?* by Alisa Childers and enhanced by her video teaching. Each session has the following sections:

- A few introductory paragraphs to set the stage for what the session is all about.

- **Leader's Note:** This brief introductory section suggests goals for the discussion time with group facilitators.

- **Read:** These are the chapters from *Another Gospel?* that participants should read before the meeting.

- **Watch:** This section spells out the points you should be listening for in the video teaching session.

- **Discuss:** These thirteen to fourteen questions will aid group discussion. They are designed to go along with the chapters you read, but even participants who haven't read the chapters ahead of time should be able to join a meaningful discussion around them. The last several questions are based on passages from the New Living Translation of the Bible, which we've printed for you right in the book. All you really need to bring each week is this study guide and your copy of *Another Gospel?* But if you want to bring a Bible or read from a different translation, that's fine too.

- **Key quotes:** Taken directly from *Another Gospel?*, these quotes are interspersed throughout the text to remind you of what you've read. You may want to read some of them aloud during your small group time to add richness and depth to the discussion.

- **Pray:** Both suggestions for prayer time and a written prayer are offered, so you can use either to close if you wish. Ideally you'll leave some time to share prayer requests so your group members can be supported in prayer as you journey together through this study.

- **Reflect:** These questions will help you reflect on what you discussed and what it means for you personally. Don't skip over these sections; they will help you process your faith journey in relation to the important doctrines of the Christian faith. We study not just to gain knowledge; we want to respond to what we've learned so that our lives are transformed.

- **Prepare:** Think about these questions as you read the assigned chapters for your next session. They will help you know where you're going next so you don't get lost along the way.

Tips for Leaders

If you're reading this section, it's likely that you've either signed up to lead a group through the *Another Gospel? DVD Experience* or you're thinking about doing so. That's great! Your willingness to serve and lead in this way will help others in their search for truth and will also grow your own faith.

We've done everything we can to make your job as easy as possible. As long as you are willing to spend a few hours reading through the chapters ahead of time, affirm the basic message of the study, can press Play on the video, and are able to keep the discussion moving through the questions, you're perfectly qualified to be a leader. Here are a few tips and tricks:

1. **Come prepared.** It probably goes without saying, but you need to set the example in spending the time to read and underline pertinent points in the chapters of *Another Gospel?* so you can lead a meaningful discussion. You should be the most prepared person in the room, able to point out pages in the book that are relevant to what's being discussed and to answer a question if the group gets stuck. It would be best if you

read the entire book before the first meeting and then reread the assigned chapters for each week along with the rest of your group. In addition, take some time before each meeting to study the Scriptures listed at the end of the session. Your time in God's Word will help enhance the group's study and yield additional insights that everyone can benefit from.

2. **Be honest.** If you're not willing to be vulnerable in answering questions, chances are good that no one else will be either. There is no shame in having doubts or questions—that's how we mature in our faith. Your honest grappling with your faith will encourage others to interact deeply with these important issues.

3. **You don't need to be an expert.** Some of these issues are complex, and no one expects you to be a Bible scholar. If you don't know something, maybe someone else in the group will. But it's okay—and a sign of good leadership—to say, "I don't know; let me find out for next week." Or even better, "Let's all see if we can find the answer to that for next week." There are many resources available to help you answer any questions your group may have.

4. **Keep the discussion on track.** There is nothing more frustrating for members than to waste group time by running down a rabbit trail. And the topics covered in *Another Gospel?* offer a lot of opportunity for

tangential discussions. Have some sentences ready for these moments: "That's a great point, and I'd love to keep discussing it, but let's table that until after the meeting so we can get through all these questions."

5. **Don't let one person dominate the discussion.** As we all know, the world is made up of introverts and extroverts, and both types of people have wise words to offer in a discussion. However, extroverts don't always notice when they're talking too much, and introverts sometimes wait for a long silence before they are ready to speak. Make space for all personalities to be comfortable sharing, and don't force people to share beyond their comfort level.

6. **Pray.** This is the best thing you can do for your group. Pray before the meeting, bringing each group member before the Lord and asking him to reveal himself to them. Pray at the end of the meeting, reminding people that ultimately the best place to go with our questions is to the throne of God. And be sure to ask for prayer requests and pray for one another throughout the week so your group can really bond.

Is Your Faith Ready for the Storm?

Sometimes we're warned about a coming storm in advance. Meteorologists see the signs and tell us to buy enough food to last a few days and hunker down in a safe place. Occasionally they're wrong, and all we end up with are empty grocery shelves, a few clouds, and a quarter inch of rain. We're thankful for good weather and glad we don't have to go to the store for a few days.

Other times a storm seems to come out of nowhere, and we find ourselves drenched and disoriented, with no shelter in sight. Maybe we come out with nothing more than wet jeans and soggy shoes, or maybe we barely escape with our lives. Either way, we wish we had been more prepared for bad weather, and we promise ourselves that we will bring a poncho next time we go hiking.

Assaults on our faith sometimes come with a warning siren—we know this or that Bible teacher has a reputation for weird theology. We read a post from our favorite social media influencer and can immediately tell that they have gone off the spiritual deep end. We don't want to be seen as close-minded or judgmental, so we don't say anything, but we secretly decide to store up theological knowledge and study our Bible so we know what we believe and why.

Other times we are blindsided by a beloved pastor who starts sharing his doubts or offering ideas that sound a little "off," but we aren't sure what's wrong with what he's saying. We didn't expect to have to defend the Bible or our faith in church, of all places. Yet that's where progressive theology is flourishing. It's in our pews and pulpits, in bestselling Christian self-help books, and on our Instagram feed. One day it will likely come to your dinner table—your daughter will pick it up at her Christian college or your best friend will carry it in along with the salad.

Whenever and however your faith storm comes, you need to be ready for it. That's where the book *Another Gospel?* and this accompanying small group guide come in. In the next six weeks you'll walk alongside other small group members as you explore the tenets of the Christian faith and discover the firm foundation they stand on. You'll learn to spot the warning signs of a coming faith storm and find the right Bible passages to shelter you from flawed arguments and false teachings. You'll identify the vulnerable spots in your belief system and rebuild the areas that weren't built quite right the first time around. And in the end, you'll emerge from the storm knowing what you believe and why.

Your guide in this journey is Alisa Childers, who faced her own faith storm and came out stronger. This book is intended to be a lifeboat for people just like you, whether you're simply looking for vocabulary to tuck away and have handy for your discussions with other believers or are already feeling adrift in a sea of doubt and about to be pulled under.

You don't need to come to this study with an extensive theological background. You don't *need* to have a lot of questions or doubts. You don't even have to know why you were invited to this small group in the first place. All you need is a desire to learn—to learn what Christianity is really about and the threats to people's faith. And hopefully, a desire to learn more about yourself and the God of the Bible.

Leader's Note

Since this is your first session together, your main goal is to get everyone comfortable sharing with the group. The secondary goal is to help group members think about where they are in their own faith journey and to be motivated to prepare for a storm.

Some people won't have read the chapters before your meeting and that's okay—we'll catch them up in the video and they can still respond to the questions. But do encourage everyone to read the suggested chapters from the book before your next meeting because they will get so much more out of your time together if they come prepared.

The progressive wave that slammed me against the Rock of Ages had broken apart my deeply ingrained assumptions about Jesus, God, and the Bible. But that same Rock of Ages slowly but surely began to rearrange the pieces, discarding a few and putting the right ones back where they belonged.

Another Gospel?, page 9

Read

Chapters 1 and 2 ("Crisis of Faith" and "The Rocks in My Shoes") in *Another Gospel?*

Watch Video Session 1

Listen for answers to the following questions, and jot down a few notes to help you remember what you heard.

- What factors led to Alisa's faith storm?

- What life experiences have influenced your faith? Where are you in your faith journey?

Discuss

Work through the following questions with your group. Make sure to leave enough time to really dig into questions 8 through 13 (those are the ones that include Scripture) and to spend a few minutes in prayer.

1. Share with the group an experience you've had in the church (camps and retreats count too) that you would consider a "spiritual high." Did that experience have lasting effects, or did it turn out to not have much substance?

2. Alisa describes growing up in the church but having a faith that was "intellectually weak and untested" with "no frame of reference or toolbox to draw from when every belief I had been so sure of was called into question" (pages 5–6). Meanwhile, her pastor calls

himself a "hopeful agnostic" (page 6). How would you describe your faith? What doctrines of Christian faith are a little confusing to you or have you not fully thought through?

If "my truth" says pork is the new kale, the consequences of that idea will bear out in reality—despite how strongly I may feel about it. My feelings about bacon won't change what it's doing to my heart, my blood pressure, and my thighs. This is why "my truth" is a myth. There is no such thing. Bacon is either good for me or it's not (or it's somewhere in between, please God!). And what I believe about it can have life or death consequences.

Likewise, as I navigated through my faith crisis, I realized that it's not enough to simply know the facts anymore . . . we have to learn how to think them through—to assess information and come to reasonable conclusions after engaging religious ideas logically and intellectually. We can't allow truth to be sacrificed on the altar of our feelings. We can't allow our fear of offending others to prevent us from warning them that they're about to step in front of a bus. Truth matters for bacon eaters, and truth matters for Christians.

Another Gospel?, page 11

3. In what ways is "the Christian worldview . . . the only one that can sufficiently explain reality" (page 10)?

4. "Deconstruction is the process of systematically dissecting and often rejecting the beliefs you grew up with. Sometimes the Christian will deconstruct all the way into atheism. Some remain there, but others experience a reconstruction. But the type of faith they end up embracing almost never resembles the Christianity they formerly knew" (page 24). Where have you seen faith deconstruction happen? Perhaps you've witnessed it in someone you know personally (don't share names or details you haven't been given permission to share, but you can describe the situation in broad terms) or a celebrity. What were some of the early warning signs? How did you feel when you heard their story?

> *I wanted to progress in my faith . . . in my understanding of God's Word, my ability to live it out, and my relationship with Jesus. But I didn't want to progress beyond truth. Once I was put through my own type of deconstruction, I wanted to reconstruct my faith by planting my flag on the firm bedrock of truth.*
>
> *Another Gospel?*, page 25

5. Alisa makes a distinction between *growing in our faith* and *growing beyond our faith*. How can you distinguish between the two?

The Christian life is never a straight trajectory of growth. We experience ups and downs on our faith journey, and as we walk forward we pick up some "rocks in our shoes"—things that lurk around the edges of our consciousness and bother us but don't seem big enough to bother taking the time and energy to dig them out of our shoes. We hope they'll just go away, and usually we can ignore them for a while. But eventually there are just too many of them, and we can't take another step until we deal with the little things that, when taken as a whole, become big things.

6. What are the rocks in your shoes? What little things bother you or make you have just a little bit of doubt or disillusionment?

7. One of the struggles Alisa describes is trying to figure out whether she is just being judgmental and close-minded or whether she is struggling against false teaching. How do you discern between those in your own life?

There is a tension between faith and doubt, between the truth we believe (or want to believe) and the experiences of life that so often don't match up to the promises of God. The fact is, the Bible tells us that our life experience isn't the way it's supposed to be—we should be disappointed by life because we were made to worship a holy God in a perfect world, and instead we find ourselves struggling against sin in a broken one.

If you're wondering if it's okay to express disappointment in God or doubt about what he says, you don't have to look further than the Bible to discover that such feelings are universal to human experience and even a necessary part of the Christian journey. A surprising number of passages in the Bible express doubt, disillusionment, and despair.

Read Psalm 77:1-15 aloud:

I cry out to God; yes, I shout.
  Oh, that God would listen to me!
When I was in deep trouble,
  I searched for the Lord.
All night long I prayed, with hands lifted toward heaven,
  but my soul was not comforted.
I think of God, and I moan,
  overwhelmed with longing for his help.

You don't let me sleep.
  I am too distressed even to pray!
I think of the good old days,
  long since ended,
when my nights were filled with joyful songs.
  I search my soul and ponder the difference now.
Has the Lord rejected me forever?
  Will he never again be kind to me?
Is his unfailing love gone forever?
  Have his promises permanently failed?
Has God forgotten to be gracious?
  Has he slammed the door on his compassion?

And I said, "This is my fate;
  the Most High has turned his hand against me."
But then I recall all you have done, O LORD;
  I remember your wonderful deeds of long ago.
They are constantly in my thoughts.
  I cannot stop thinking about your mighty works.

O God, your ways are holy.
　Is there any god as mighty as you?
You are the God of great wonders!
　You demonstrate your awesome power among the
　　nations.
By your strong arm, you redeemed your people,
　the descendants of Jacob and Joseph.

8. Which of the psalmist's emotions and experiences can you relate to? Describe the circumstances surrounding those feelings in your life. Which feelings expressed in this psalm have not been part of your faith journey yet?

9. The turning point in this psalm comes in verse 11: "But then I recall . . ." What changes for the psalmist?

10. How can you apply what the psalmist learned about dealing with and eventually overcoming doubt to your own life?

Read Hebrews 10:19-25 aloud:

> And so, dear brothers and sisters, we can boldly enter
> heaven's Most Holy Place because of the blood of Jesus.
> By his death, Jesus opened a new and life-giving way
> through the curtain into the Most Holy Place. And since
> we have a great High Priest who rules over God's house,
> let us go right into the presence of God with sincere
> hearts fully trusting him. For our guilty consciences have
> been sprinkled with Christ's blood to make us clean, and
> our bodies have been washed with pure water.
>
> Let us hold tightly without wavering to the hope
> we affirm, for God can be trusted to keep his promise.
> Let us think of ways to motivate one another to acts
> of love and good works. And let us not neglect our
> meeting together, as some people do, but encourage
> one another, especially now that the day of his return is
> drawing near.

11. These words were written to believers who were
    struggling against assaults on their faith from within
    the church and also enduring great personal suffering.
    In other words, they had good reason to struggle with
    doubt. What Christian practices or disciplines does the
    passage list that can help us hold on to the hope we
    have in Christ?

12. Which of these actions have helped you most? Which ones do you want to make use of more often?

13. What practical action will you take in the next week to "hold tightly without wavering to the hope [you] affirm"?

Pray

Close your time together in prayer. If time allows, take prayer requests or break into smaller groups of two to three people to pray for one another. Otherwise, simply close with a simple prayer like the one below:

Dear heavenly Father,

We acknowledge that life on earth is full of experiences that can easily make us doubt your goodness and your love—and sometimes even your very existence. We want to believe, so we ask that in the next six weeks you will remove the scales from our eyes and enable us to see the truth. Help our unbelief and draw us closer to yourself. We want to know the truth, and we want to know you.

Amen.

[Christianity is] deeply rooted in history. In fact, it is the only religious system I can think of that depends on a historical event (the resurrection of Jesus) being real—not fake—news.

Another Gospel?, page 10

Reflect

Before the next group meeting, spend some time reflecting on what you have learned about your faith.

- What do you hope to get out of your study of *Another Gospel?*

- What are some new ideas or questions that the first session has brought to mind for you—things you haven't considered before and now would like to find answers to?

- What things make you doubt God or doubt what he reveals about himself in the Bible? Pray that the Lord will reveal the truth about these things in the coming weeks.

Fill out a Belief Inventory:
Answer the following questions about what you believe about key Christian doctrines. Be honest with yourself. The answers are just for you, and this exercise will be valuable and helpful only if you are willing to face the truth about what you believe. At the end of the six-week study, you'll look back at this inventory and see if any of your answers have changed.

On a scale from 1 to 10, how equipped are you to deal with assaults on core Christian doctrines?

1   2   3   4   5   6   7   8   9   10

1—I think I'm a Christian, but please don't ask me any questions.

5—I know the answers to some things but not to others.

7—I enjoy conversations about faith. Even if I don't have all the answers, I love to be challenged to learn more.

10—I love it when people ask questions and debate because I think I have good answers.

Which of these statements best describes what you believe about Christianity?

☐ I don't doubt any of the core tenets of the Christian faith. This book study isn't really something I personally need; it's just something I'm interested in to equip me to help others.

☐ I'm a Christian, but sometimes I have questions and doubts about core issues. I hope this study can answer some of my questions.

☐ My beliefs are a hodgepodge; I no longer believe a lot of what most Christians believe.

Which of these statements best fits what you believe about the Bible?

☐ It's the inerrant Word of God, the basis for everything I believe about God and live by.

☐ It documents what ancient Jews and Christians believed about God; some parts are outdated or don't apply anymore.

☐ It's a human book, edifying but not authoritative or inspired.

Which of these statements best fits what you believe about Creation?

☐ Everything was created by God with a word.

☐ I'm open to believing that God used macroevolution to create the world.

☐ Scientific evidence says that everything evolved over a long period of time without divine assistance; the biblical account is an ancient way of explaining things biblical writers couldn't understand, and it shouldn't be taken literally.

☐ I don't know what I believe.

Which of these statements best fits what you believe about sin?

☐ I prefer terms like *brokenness* or *weakness* that don't sound so harsh.

☐ There isn't really a one-size-fits-all definition of sin; what is wrong for you might not be wrong for me.

☐ Sin is an offense against God that causes separation from him and is thus the biggest problem humans have, the source of all suffering.

Which of these statements best fits what you believe about absolute truth?

☐ The Bible is the standard for absolute truth.

☐ The Bible contains some truths, but isn't *the* objective standard for truth.

☐ The Bible is helpful, but there are no "sacred cows."

☐ It is arrogant to claim that any particular belief is better or worse than any other.

Which of these statements best fits what you believe about miracles?

☐ God can do anything, and the miracles recorded in the Bible truly happened as they are recorded.

☐ God can do anything, but many of the miracles recorded in the Bible didn't necessarily happen.

☐ The miracles recorded in the Bible were invented to make people believe the Jewish/Christian faith.

Which of these statements best fits what you believe about Jesus?

☐ He was a great religious leader.

☐ He is the Son of God, the Messiah promised throughout Scripture who delivers us from sin.

☐ I'm not sure who he was or why it matters.

Which of these statements best fits what you believe about the cross of Christ?

☐ It is a historical event that makes it possible for anyone who believes in Jesus to be saved for all eternity from sin and death; Jesus' death on the cross in my place makes me righteous in God's sight.

☐ It is a historical event, but it was only the death of a religious figure due to the powerful leaders of the day. It is a good example of forgiveness but doesn't have any significance beyond that.

☐ It doesn't matter if it really happened or not.

Which of these statements best fits what you believe about the resurrection of Christ?

☐ It was the completion of Christ's work that saves me and the foretaste of the resurrection that all believers will one day experience through him.

☐ It didn't happen; the disciples made it up because they couldn't face the fact that he had died.

☐ It doesn't matter whether it was a physical or merely a spiritual resurrection. It's what we learn from the story that matters.

☐ I don't know if it happened or not.

Which of these statements best fits what you believe about the Christian faith?

☐ It is a primitive set of beliefs developed by primitive people.

☐ It's time to move beyond the ancient ideas, taking the best of Christianity and getting rid of what is outdated.

☐ It summarizes the truth about the creation of the world, the fall of humankind, salvation through Christ, and the way to eternal life.

Which of these statements best fits what you believe about judgment?

☐ When Jesus returns, he will judge every person; Christians will be declared righteous, and evil will be punished.

☐ It is something Christians made up to motivate people to behave better.

☐ It is evidence that God is petty and vindictive.

Which of these statements best fits what you believe about yourself?

☐ I don't believe there will be a Judgment Day.

☐ I'm a pretty good person, so I'm not too worried about Judgment Day.

☐ I'm a very bad person, so I'm very worried about what will happen to me on Judgment Day.

☐ I'm a sinner, but I'm saved by God's grace and have nothing to fear on Judgment Day.

Which of these statements best fits what you believe about hell?

☐ It's a real place, and people who don't believe in Jesus for salvation will spend eternity there.

☐ It's really just a metaphor for separation from God.

☐ It is nothing more than the consequences we experience now for the bad choices we make here on earth.

☐ A good God couldn't create hell, so therefore it doesn't exist.

Which of these statements best fits what you believe about faith?

☐ It is a blind leap in the dark.

☐ Faith is 100 percent certainty about something.

☐ Faith is trust based on reasonable evidence.

Which of these statements best fits what you believe about doubt?

☐ It is a great thing—a mark of intelligence and something we should strive to exhibit.

☐ It is sinful.

☐ It arises in the context of faith and, if dealt with appropriately, can lead to growth and greater understanding.

Prepare

If you weren't able to read chapters 1 and 2 in *Another Gospel?* before this week's meeting, read those this week. They set the stage for the entire book and thus provide an important foundation you won't want to miss.

Session 2 covers chapters 3 and 4, "Creeds, Cobbler, and Walter Bauer" and "Fixing What Isn't Broken." Read those chapters in preparation for your next meeting. As you read, think about these questions:

- What things do most Christians agree about?

- What are the most frequently cited issues for why people struggle with or even leave the church?

Session 2

Are Your Roots Deep Enough?

You don't have to be an expert gardener to know that a plant is only as healthy as its root system. There's nothing like pulling up a dying plant and exposing its parched and shriveled roots to convince you that proper planting, watering, and sunlight are essential for growth.

The same holds true for our faith. If our spiritual roots are shallow and undeveloped, our faith won't grow, we won't bear spiritual fruit, and eventually our faith will die. In the parable of the farmer scattering seed, only the seed that landed in fertile soil grew and produced a crop. The seed along the path, among the rocks, and amidst the thorns did not grow because it couldn't put down roots (Luke 8:4-15). Simply put, the only way we can be saved is by having roots firmly planted in Christ.

But that's more difficult than it sounds, isn't it? Along the path of life we encounter threats to our faith. Some of these come from the outside, from the prevailing winds of culture or even the arguments of self-proclaimed Christians that poke holes in the tenets of our faith like pesky insects eating a young plant. Other hazards are internal—doubts and trials that give way to unbelief like a disease that eats away at the fruit before it has a chance to grow. Regardless of the source of our trouble, we have to clear out everything that hinders growth, prune away the dead branches, and expose ourselves to the living water so we can grow deep, stable roots.

In this session we'll examine the essentials for true faith and the threats that assault it. The goal is to allow space for genuine doubt that can lead to growth while not nurturing unbelief. We need to know what and why we believe so we can successfully weather the storms and droughts that will undoubtedly come.

Leader's Note

Hopefully group members have read the chapters this week and are starting to open up and share with authenticity. Your main goal this week is to create a safe environment in which to define the core issues of the Christian faith and acknowledge the questions that need to be addressed. Doubts and barriers to faith should be met with respect and love and then gently countered with biblical truth. Ask for God's help to discern and rightly respond to the true issues behind group members' questions and struggles.

> I think it's time for another reformation. Not a reformation that progresses beyond historic Christianity. Not one that looks down on these early believers as less enlightened and more primitive in their understanding of God, but one that rediscovers the very definition of Christianity.
>
> *Another Gospel?*, page 40

Read

Chapters 3 and 4 ("Creeds, Cobbler, and Walter Bauer" and "Fixing What Isn't Broken") in *Another Gospel?*

Watch Video Session 2

In this video, Alisa and J. Warner Wallace, author of *Person of Interest*, discuss how early Christianity affirmed a core set of beliefs. Then Alisa invites Jon McCray, popular apologist for the YouTube channel *Whaddo You Meme??* to talk about his experience with progressive Christianity. Jot down a few notes to help you remember what you hear in these discussions.

- What are some of the core beliefs that early Christians affirmed (1 Corinthians 15:3-5)?

Importance of Creeds to Combat heresy

Apostle's Creed - Needed especially today

Arianism - Jesus is "created being by the Father, not eternal.

- Why do some find progressive ideas about Christianity appealing?

- What are some reasons to affirm and hold on to the beliefs of historic Christianity?

- Why do you believe Christianity is true?

Discuss

Work through the following questions with your group. Be sure to leave enough time to really dig into questions 8 through 13 (the ones that include Scripture) and to spend a few minutes in prayer.

1. What assumptions did you grow up with that you now realize are not elements of essential doctrines? How do you think you picked up the idea that these things were part of the Christian faith?

   Gnosticism - live in eternity non embodied is false belief Many christians assume do to influence of culture (Greek thought)

2. What are the essentials of Christian faith? Work together as a group to come up with a succinct statement of core doctrines, referring to 1 Corinthians 15:3-5 as a starting point.

> I passed on to you what was most important and what had also been passed on to me. Christ died for our sins, just as the Scriptures said. He was buried, and he was raised from the dead on the third day, just as the Scriptures said. He was seen by Peter and then by the Twelve.
>
> 1 Corinthians 15:3-5

Part of growing up in our faith is grappling with the intersection between the circumstances of our lives and the Word of God. Because we live in the time between Christ's first coming to save us and his second coming when he will rule in perfect righteousness and justice, our lived experience often casts doubt on the promises of God. We wonder where God is when we look at the suffering in the world. We struggle to detach the failures of sinful people from our understanding of God. And we are such fickle and finite creatures that we sometimes just find it hard to hang on to our faith. These are legitimate struggles shared by every human throughout the ages, so we need to engage with them.

3. Alisa lists seven legitimate problems that tend to push people into progressivism: abuse of power, lack of a safe place to express doubt, the moral demands of historic Christianity, questions about the Bible, competing worldviews, legalism, and the problem of suffering. Which of these do you struggle with most, and which ones are not significant barriers to you?

Historically, Christians have believed that the Bible is the Word of God and that Jesus is God incarnate who died for our sins and was raised to life for our salvation. There is one thing we can be certain of: The earliest Christians—the ones who knew Jesus personally, who saw him with their own eyes and touched him with their own hands—believed the teachings laid out in the earliest creeds and New Testament writings. These aren't just modern opinions or the privileged musings of an enlightened Western civilization. . . . It should be up to Jesus and the apostles to define what Christianity is.

Another Gospel?, pages 40–41

4. How have your church and/or other faith influences (family, school, small groups, mentors, etc.) helped you grow deeper roots in the faith?

5. How have your church and/or other faith influences hindered you from growing deeper roots in the faith? (Be careful not to let this turn into a church-bashing session—and don't get bogged down with too much detail.)

When we are faced with immeasurable and unspeakable pain, we have a choice. We can open our hands to the Father and fall at his feet, or we can shake our fist at him and walk away. We can throw the raw magnitude of our doubts, questions, and piercing grief into his capable lap, or we can gather it all up into clenched hands and declare him incompetent . . . or nonexistent. We each have that choice.

Another Gospel?, page 66

6. When Satan tempted Eve in the Garden, his tactic (which you'll recall was very successful) was to cast doubt on God's words. "Did God really say . . ." he asked and then followed up by twisting God's commands (Genesis 3:1). When have you seen paraphrasing of theology or exaggeration used to cast doubt on the Christian faith?

7. Alisa writes, "Unbelief is a conscious choice to live as if God does not exist—and it's born out of sinful desires. Doubt, however, is *an entirely different concept*" (page 49). What is the practical difference between unbelief and doubt? How can you tell which one you are engaging in?

While progressivism often glorifies skepticism, most Christians who are struggling with doubt would rather move past their angst. It's no fun to constantly question every belief or wonder if God even exists. Fortunately, the Bible gives us a road map for growth. If we are truly seeking God, we will find him. If we really want to grow in our faith, he will help us. In fact, that's his number one goal for us.

Read Psalm 1 aloud:

> Oh, the joys of those who do not
> follow the advice of the wicked,
> or stand around with sinners,
> or join in with mockers.
> But they delight in the law of the LORD,
> meditating on it day and night.
> They are like trees planted along the riverbank,
> bearing fruit each season.
> Their leaves never wither,
> and they prosper in all they do.

But not the wicked!
   They are like worthless chaff, scattered by the wind.
They will be condemned at the time of judgment.
   Sinners will have no place among the godly.
For the LORD watches over the path of the godly,
   but the path of the wicked leads to destruction.

8. This psalm contrasts a tree with deep roots and the chaff that is blown away in the wind. According to this psalm, what are the characteristics of a tree with deep roots? How do those metaphors translate into a description of a Christian's spiritual life?

9. What happens to rootless, ungodly people?

10. Growth in our Christian walk comes from God, but there are things we are responsible to do to prepare ourselves for God's work. What do fruitful Christians do to position themselves for growth? Do you think your friends would say you exhibit these actions and characteristics?

Read John 15:1-8:

> I am the true grapevine, and my Father is the gardener.
> He cuts off every branch of mine that doesn't produce
> fruit, and he prunes the branches that do bear fruit so
> they will produce even more. You have already been
> pruned and purified by the message I have given you.
> Remain in me, and I will remain in you. For a branch
> cannot produce fruit if it is severed from the vine, and
> you cannot be fruitful unless you remain in me.
>
> Yes, I am the vine; you are the branches. Those who
> remain in me, and I in them, will produce much fruit. For
> apart from me you can do nothing. Anyone who does
> not remain in me is thrown away like a useless branch
> and withers. Such branches are gathered into a pile
> to be burned. But if you remain in me and my words
> remain in you, you may ask for anything you want, and
> it will be granted! When you produce much fruit, you are
> my true disciples. This brings great glory to my Father.

11. According to this passage, what are the responsibilities
    of the gardener? How have you seen God doing these
    things in your life?

12. In Matthew 7:20, Jesus tells us, "Just as you can identify a tree by its fruit, so you can identify people by their actions." What are the responsibilities of the branches—the Christians? How are you succeeding at taking these actions, and where do you need to repent and grow?

13. Based on John 15 and Psalm 1, what would you say are the benefits of being firmly rooted in Christ? How have you experienced these things in your own life?

Pray

Close your time together in prayer. If time allows, take prayer requests, or break into smaller groups of two to three people to pray for one another. You might model your prayer on Colossians 2:6-7 (printed after the prayer). Otherwise, simply close with a simple prayer like the one below:

Dear heavenly Father,

So many things threaten our faith or cause us to doubt. We pray that those things would not be barriers to faith, but rather would help us grow deeper in our walk with you. We acknowledge that you are the only source of truth, and so we come to you with our questions, doubts, and struggles. Give us answers to our honest cries for help. We draw near to you in faith, even as we honestly acknowledge areas of confusion.

Amen.

Reflect

Before the next group meeting, spend some time reflecting on what you have learned about deepening your faith.

- What questions or doubts did this week's discussion bring up for you? Journal and pray about them. Don't be afraid to be honest with God because he already knows what's in your heart. This is the first step to finding answers—and eventually peace and joy.

> *Just as you accepted Christ Jesus as your Lord, you must continue to follow him. Let your roots grow down into him, and let your lives be built on him. Then your faith will grow strong in the truth you were taught, and you will overflow with thankfulness.*
>
> Colossians 2:6-7

- Starting each sentence with "I believe," write down in your own words the core essentials of the faith. Refer to pages 31–33 in *Another Gospel?* or your answers to question 2 if you need help.

- What are some habits and practices you will implement this week to help grow your faith?

Prepare

Session 3 covers chapters 5 and 6, "A Different Kind of Christianity" and "Nothing New under the Sun." Read those chapters in preparation for your next meeting. As you read, think about these questions:

- What is progressive Christianity? What makes it so attractive?

- How can Christians guard against heresy?

Is This Another Gospel?

By now you're familiar with Alisa's story—how she encountered teachings in her own church that contradicted the gospel and left her confused about what she had always believed to be true about the Christian faith. Her experience is not unusual, and in fact this kind of thing was going on even in the churches planted by the apostles Peter and Paul. The issue isn't whether we will face similar questions, but when and how—and whether we will know what to do about it when that moment arrives.

False teachings—including those of progressive Christianity—make inroads in the church today because they seem to take all the best parts of our faith and leave behind anything we are a little uncomfortable with. With weakened ethical requirements and an overly open-minded posture, they appeal to our Christian sentiment of goodwill toward all. We want as many people as possible to be saved, so we can be swayed by arguments that refute judgment and hell. We want people to know God as their loving Father, so we talk about his compassion for our hurts rather than discussing his righteous judgment. And we like everyone to feel good about themselves, so we'd rather not admit we are sinners in need of a Savior. But such a faith, in addition to being contrary to the Bible, is weak and meaningless in the face of our real-life struggles against pain and suffering. It may be enough when we are sailing through life without a care, but it can't help us when we are truly in need.

In this session we'll examine the core beliefs of progressive Christianity. We'll see how these arguments are made and where they fall apart. And we'll see that they are nothing new after all—these are much like the heresy faced by Peter and Paul in the first century.

Leader's Note

Your main goal this week is to help participants understand the common false teachings of progressive Christianity and begin to see why those are such a problem. Continue to model and insist on an atmosphere of kindness and encouragement in which people will be comfortable sharing their doubts and struggles.

> *For people to deconstruct their faith—to begin pulling the thread of deeply ingrained beliefs—they had to first figure out what to do with the Bible.*
>
> *Another Gospel?*, page 78

Read

Chapters 5 and 6 ("A Different Kind of Christianity" and "Nothing New under the Sun") in *Another Gospel?*

Watch Video Session 3

In this session, Alisa and Jon McCray discuss how progressive ideas about Christianity amount to another gospel entirely. Jot down a few notes to help you remember what you heard.

- In what ways has the progressive movement within the church deviated from the essence of historic Christianity?

- What are the beliefs or dogmas that tend to unify the progressive movement?

Discuss

Work through the following questions with your group. Make sure to leave enough time to really dig into questions 8 through 14 (those are the ones that include Scripture) and to spend a few minutes in prayer.

1. Have you encountered Christians who call themselves emergent or progressive? What seemed to be the hallmarks of their faith, the things that were central to their experience and beliefs?

2. Alisa writes, "From the beginning, Christians have been in agreement that the Bible is cohesive, coherent, inspired by God, and authoritative for our lives" (page 80). Do you agree with all of these statements? Which ones do you most often see questioned by people who consider themselves Christians?

Progressive Christianity can sound like a more inclusive, perhaps kinder and gentler gospel. As people who want to love our neighbor well, we might be tempted to soften the edges of the historical doctrines of the faith and talk about spirituality, brokenness, and inclusiveness rather than using old-fashioned words like *sin*, *redemption*, and *judgment*. But when we dig a little deeper and consider the way progressives do away with the doctrines of original sin, the Cross, judgment, the Resurrection—basically everything that makes the Christian faith hold together—we are left with a vapid spirituality that doesn't solve any of our problems or provide satisfactory answers to our existential questions.

> *Progressive Christianity is not simply a shift in the Christian view of social issues. It's not simply permission to embrace messiness and authenticity in Christian life. It's not simply a response to doubt, legalism, abuse, or hypocrisy. It's an entirely different religion—with another Jesus—and another gospel.*
>
> Another Gospel?, page 76

3. "The progressive view of the Cross is that Jesus was killed by an angry mob for speaking truth to power. God didn't need his sacrifice, but in some way submitted to it in order to set an example of forgiveness for us all to follow. God didn't require blood—humans did" (page 86). Where have you encountered this viewpoint? How could you argue against it?

> *The progressive view of the Bible is to see it as primarily a human book. Most progressives see the Bible as an archaic travel journal that documents what ancient Jews and Christians believed about God. Not all of it is authoritative. Not all of it is inspired. None of it is inerrant. Sometimes, if you look really hard, you might find the word of God in it. But it's up to you to decide which parts work for you and which parts don't. This is a radical departure from the historic Christian view of the Bible . . . [and] a profound dismissal of how Jesus viewed the Scriptures.*
>
> *Another Gospel?*, pages 82–83

4. Where have Christians traditionally upheld the doctrine of original sin? What are the implications to the Christian worldview and daily life if you don't believe in the holiness of God and the innate sinfulness of humanity?

5. The rule of faith, which was the second-century summary of the apostles' teachings, is outlined on page 91 of *Another Gospel?* These beliefs encompass the message of the gospel, which follows the narrative arc of Creation, the Fall, redemption, and restoration. Looking at that list, explain why each one is essential

for the coherence of the Christian faith. In other words, why can you not just pick the ones that make the most sense to you?

6. Brian McLaren's progressive version of the gospel is found on page 92 of *Another Gospel?* Reread it. What does it say about the fundamental problem facing humanity and the solution to that problem? How is this false gospel insufficient when you are standing at the grave of someone you love, trying to come to terms with their death?

> *Even in our churches, truth and lies can be wedged in like sardines, leaving many Christians confused and discouraged.*
> *Another Gospel?*, pages 96–97

The progressive movement is really just a new name for some old heresies. It seeks to either add something to the gospel or take something away so that it suits us better. Like the circumcision party, it says that we need "Jesus plus works," which is often framed within the context of social justice. Like the Gnostics, it says we need "Jesus plus new knowledge." Like the Marcionites, it says we need "Jesus minus judgment, hell, and the Old Testament."

7. What is it about each of the "Jesus plus" or "Jesus minus" heresies that appeals to people? How does each differ from the true gospel of Jesus Christ?

Read Matthew 7:13-23:

> You can enter God's Kingdom only through the narrow gate. The highway to hell is broad, and its gate is wide for the many who choose that way. But the gateway to life is very narrow and the road is difficult, and only a few ever find it.
>
> Beware of false prophets who come disguised as harmless sheep but are really vicious wolves. You can identify them by their fruit, that is, by the way they act. Can you pick grapes from thornbushes, or figs from thistles? A good tree produces good fruit, and a bad tree produces bad fruit. A good tree can't produce bad fruit, and a bad tree can't produce good fruit. So every tree that does not produce good fruit is chopped down and

thrown into the fire. Yes, just as you can identify a tree by its fruit, so you can identify people by their actions.

Not everyone who calls out to me, "Lord! Lord!" will enter the Kingdom of Heaven. Only those who actually do the will of my Father in heaven will enter. On judgment day many will say to me, "Lord! Lord! We prophesied in your name and cast out demons in your name and performed many miracles in your name." But I will reply, "I never knew you. Get away from me, you who break God's laws."

8. Based on this passage, what makes the road to salvation difficult?

9. The false prophets are disguised and thus difficult to pick out at first. What is it that makes them seem like legitimate Christian teachers? What specific things might a false teacher do or say in today's churches that would make them difficult to identify?

10. How can we recognize false teachers despite their disguises? What practical methods or tests can you use to distinguish a false teacher who looks harmless from a teacher who is preaching the true gospel?

Read 2 Peter 2:1-3, 12-22:

But there were also false prophets in Israel, just as there will be false teachers among you. They will cleverly teach destructive heresies and even deny the Master who bought them. In this way, they will bring sudden destruction on themselves. Many will follow their evil teaching and shameful immorality. And because of these teachers, the way of truth will be slandered. In their greed they will make up clever lies to get hold of your money. But God condemned them long ago, and their destruction will not be delayed. . . .

These false teachers are like unthinking animals, creatures of instinct, born to be caught and destroyed. They scoff at things they do not understand, and like animals, they will be destroyed. Their destruction is their reward for the harm they have done. They love to indulge in evil pleasures in broad daylight. They are a disgrace and a stain among you. They delight in deception even as they eat with you in your fellowship meals. They commit adultery with their eyes, and their desire for sin is never satisfied. They lure unstable people into sin, and they are well trained in greed. They live under God's curse. They have wandered off the right road and followed the footsteps of Balaam son of Beor, who loved to earn money by doing wrong. But Balaam was stopped from his mad course when his donkey rebuked him with a human voice.

These people are as useless as dried-up springs or as mist blown away by the wind. They are doomed to blackest darkness. They brag about themselves with empty, foolish boasting. With an appeal to twisted sexual desires, they lure back into sin those who have barely escaped from a lifestyle of deception. They promise freedom, but they themselves are slaves of sin and corruption. For you are a slave to whatever controls you. And when people escape from the wickedness of the world by knowing our Lord and Savior Jesus Christ and then get tangled up and enslaved by sin again, they are worse off than before. It would be better if they had never known the way to righteousness than to know it and then reject the command they were given to live a holy life. They prove the truth of this proverb: "A dog returns to its vomit." And another says, "A washed pig returns to the mud."

11. This is a big passage to unpack, and we obviously don't have time to do it justice, but it paints a vivid picture of false teachers. What are some of the characteristics of false teachers that stand out to you? How have you

seen false teachers exhibit these characteristics on their platforms (whether in person or online)?

12. Based on this passage, why is Peter so concerned about the false teaching in his church? Why is it such a significant problem?

13. Based on this list, what makes false teaching so alluring? Where do you see these features in progressive Christianity?

14. What are some of the images used to describe false teachers, and what is going to happen to them? How do these illustrations expand your understanding of false teachers?

Pray

Close your time together in prayer. If time allows, take prayer requests, or break into smaller groups of two to three people to pray for one another. Otherwise, simply close with a simple prayer like the one below:

Dear heavenly Father,

It's easy to get muddled about what we believe when someone confronts us with arguments that sound good. We're seeking the truth. Help us to know what we believe and why we believe it. When faced with false teachings, help us discern between truth and error. When confronted with doubts, help us stand firm in the truth of the gospel of Jesus Christ. When battered by disappointment, bind up our wounds and draw us near. Show us the beautiful, glorious gospel and grant faith to our faltering hearts.

Amen.

Reflect

Before the next group meeting, spend some time reflecting on what you have learned about progressive Christianity.

> *Just because our culture has come to a consensus on something does not make it true or right.*
>
> *Another Gospel?*, page 110

- What questions did this week's discussion bring up for you? Journal and pray about them.

- Journal about your experiences with false teachers or your struggle to identify them. Have you been following some teachers whom you now think you should perhaps "unfollow"? What is it about their teaching that you're beginning to see does not match the true gospel? Look back at the passages you discussed from Matthew and 2 Peter and ask yourself (and the Lord, in prayer) if there are specific things these teachers seem to be doing or saying that identify them as false teachers.

- What are some habits and practices you will implement this week to help you stand firm in your faith against "wolves in sheep's clothing" who try to deceive you with clever words?

Prepare

Session 4 is a little longer than the last two sessions, so you'll want to leave plenty of time for preparation. It covers chapters 7 through 9, "For the Bible Tells Me So?"; "Was It True Only for Them?"; and "Authority Problems." Read those chapters in preparation for your next meeting. As you read, think about these questions:

- What makes the Bible reliable and trustworthy?

- Why is it reasonable to order my life under the authority of the Bible?

What Is Ultimately Trustworthy?

It all hinges on the Bible. In the words of the Westminster Confession of Faith, the Bible is "given by inspiration of God to be the rule of faith and life." As we see in Romans 1, there are things we can learn about God and the world by observing creation. This is what theologians call natural revelation. However, without the Bible we don't have what theologians call special revelation, which gives us the specifics of who God is and his plan of salvation. Nor do we have hope of eternal life, because without the biblical account we can't know Jesus, the author and perfecter of our faith and the only one who can reconcile us to God. Whether or not we can trust the Bible is vitally important.

Fortunately, our trust in the Bible is not blind. In fact,

there is far more textual evidence for the reliability of the Bible than for any other ancient work of literature. And there is ample evidence for Jesus' life, death, and resurrection. Our faith is not based on a fairy tale or a single ancient manuscript—it is based on multiple, independent historical accounts and eyewitness testimony, all of which point to Jesus Christ being the Son of God who died for our salvation. And very smart people have been studying and recording these issues for two thousand years.

This week we'll enter into the world of scholars and theologians and detectives—people trained in the art and science of differentiating between truth and falsehood. You'll begin to see why so many intelligent people believe with all their hearts that the Bible is God's Word and the authoritative source for our knowledge of God. At the end of it all, you'll have some new strategies for studying these historical works, a few logical arguments to back up your faith in the God of the Bible, and hopefully a renewed love for Scripture. The Bible is the living and active Word of God, able to light the way to true life through Jesus Christ.

Leader's Note

This week we're covering quite a bit of ground, but don't be intimidated. The study has been designed to be just as manageable as all the other weeks. Your main goal this week is to help participants see the beautiful truth of God's Word. Don't let the group get bogged down in secondary issues—focus on the Bible and all the logical reasons we have for trusting its authenticity.

> *The earliest Christians had no possible motivation for making the whole thing up. In fact, they would have had every reason to recant under threat of death and torture. But they didn't. Because it was all true.*
>
> *Another Gospel?*, page 137

Read

Chapters 7 through 9 ("For the Bible Tells Me So?"; "Was It True Only for Them?"; and "Authority Problems") in *Another Gospel?*

Watch Video Session 4

In this session, Alisa and J. Warner Wallace discuss the evidence that points to the reliability and trustworthiness of the Bible. Listen for answers to the following questions, and jot down a few notes to help you remember what you heard.

- Do we have an accurate copy of the original Bible texts? How can we be sure?

- What reasons do we have to trust that the biblical account accurately portrays the truth about Jesus, his life, and his teachings?

- Why do you believe the Bible is true?

Discuss

Work through the following questions with your group. Make sure to leave enough time to really dig into questions 9 through 14 (those are the ones that include Scripture) and to spend a few minutes in prayer.

1. What was your earliest experience with the Bible? How would you characterize your current experience with or attitude toward God's Word?

If progressive Christianity starts with dismantling the Bible, we need to know if the Scriptures we hold in our hands are truly reliable. How can we know this is God's Word? What if time and the errors or biases of scribes corrupted what God intended? And how can we deal with all the differences in various manuscripts—don't they mean we can't trust the words in our Bible? Thankfully, there are very good, logical reasons to have confidence in our Bibles.

> *The New Testament has more copies and earlier copies than any work of ancient classical literature.*
>
> *Another Gospel?*, page 128

2. One of the primary ways scholars assess the reliability of the Bible is by textual criticism. In just a few sentences, describe what textual criticism is. How can this type of scholarship give us confidence in the biblical text? Why can textual variants actually increase our confidence in the Bible?

3. Alisa reminds us that all scholars have biases. The important thing is to recognize them so you are not taken in by false arguments. What are some strategies you can use to identify a scholar's or critic's bias? What are some common biases among progressive or liberal theologians?

What theologians refer to as progressive revelation [is] "progressive" in the sense that God continued to reveal more information to human beings as time went on. But it doesn't mean that the revelation progressed from error to truth. In this way, there is a huge difference between what theologians have historically meant by progressive revelation and what progressive Christians mean. The main difference is that the progressive revelation we find in Scripture never contradicts itself, and the revelation of God culminates in Jesus Christ. . . . Jesus is God's final word. Progressive revelation is like bricks stacked on top of one another forming a wall of a building. Progressive theology, by contrast, says that we started with the wrong bricks, so we need to remove them and put other ones in—or tear the whole wall down and start over.

Another Gospel?, pages 138–139

4. Give an example of progressive revelation in Scripture. How is that different from progressive theology?

Wipinjart enelly Men, women & Children is God's will. Having More than one wife. Slavery

5. Progressive theology implies that the Bible represents Christianity in its infancy and that because we know more now than the early Christians did, we can and should look back at what was written, analyze what they believed, and adjust or even disagree with what they taught. What is wrong with this line of reasoning?

6. What are some of the strategies historians use to determine if the events recorded in a work of literature are real events or fictional stories? According to these metrics, what evidence do we have that the Gospels are eyewitness accounts of true historical events?

P. 140 ff.
Focus is on Gospel Accounts

The dating [of the Gospels] suggests not only that the Gospels were written by people who were alive when Jesus was, but also that the books themselves were written with razor-sharp accuracy when it comes to historical details.

Another Gospel?, page 141

If the gospel was fabricated by a bunch of first-century Jewish men, their tendency would be to simplify, unify, clarify, and beautify Jesus' sayings—to make Christianity much broader, easier, and more pleasant. But they didn't because it's not broad, easy, or pleasant. It's incredibly difficult. It's described as a narrow road that few people actually find.

Another Gospel?, pages 144–145

7. The Gospel accounts have certain variations between them. What accounts for the differences? How do the variations actually make them more believable rather than less believable?

4 Personality Types

8. Alisa writes, "Progressives find Scripture compelling. The difference is that, rather than viewing it as the authoritative Word from God to people, they see

the Bible as an antiquated library of books that we can examine like ancient relics . . . our spiritual ancestors' best attempts to understand God in their own cultures, using whatever knowledge they had at the time . . . our predecessors' spiritual travel journal" (page 155). How would viewing the Bible that way affect a person's spiritual walk?

There are many reasons we should read and study Scripture, but it will be difficult to gain any of the benefits if we think of the Bible merely as a past record of what less spiritually evolved people believed hundreds or thousands of years ago. If we don't come to the understanding that the Bible is God's Word, we won't believe we have to obey what it says—and in time, we may not bother reading it at all. But if we have come to believe that these are the words of life, we will share the attitudes of David, Paul, Jesus, and countless Christians through the ages who all believed and lived as if every word of Scripture is a word from God himself.

Read Psalm 19:7-11:

The instructions of the LORD are perfect,
    reviving the soul.
The decrees of the LORD are trustworthy,
    making wise the simple.

The commandments of the LORD are right,
  bringing joy to the heart.
The commands of the LORD are clear,
  giving insight for living.
Reverence for the LORD is pure,
  lasting forever.
The laws of the LORD are true;
  each one is fair.
They are more desirable than gold,
  even the finest gold.
They are sweeter than honey,
  even honey dripping from the comb.
They are a warning to your servant,
  a great reward for those who obey them.

9. How does David, the author of Psalm 19, view God's Word? Unpack the images and adjectives he uses to describe it.

10. How does his attitude compare to yours—in what ways do you love God's Word and in what ways are you ambivalent or skeptical of it?

11. According to this passage, what are the benefits of reading and studying Scripture? How does it change us?

In years past, it was assumed that if you called yourself a Christian, you believed in biblical authority. But now as progressive Christianity infiltrates and infects the true church, we all must decide: How much authority does this book hold in our lives? To inform our view of the Bible, we can choose to follow the whims of a godless culture or we can choose to follow Jesus. I choose Jesus.

Another Gospel?, page 176

Read 2 Timothy 3:14-17:

You must remain faithful to the things you have been taught. You know they are true, for you know you can trust those who taught you. You have been taught the holy Scriptures from childhood, and they have given you the wisdom to receive the salvation that comes by trusting in Christ Jesus. All Scripture is inspired by God and is useful to teach us what is true and to make us realize what is wrong in our lives. It corrects us when we are wrong and teaches us to do what is right. God uses it to prepare and equip his people to do every good work.

12. Based on this passage, what are the purposes of Scripture?

13. How has Scripture done these things in your life? Give specific examples of how God has done his work in and through you as you've read and studied the Bible.

14. Going forward, how do you think this week's study will change the way you view, use, and feel about Scripture? (Think back to how you answered question 1 on page 68.)

Pray

Close your time together in prayer. If time allows, take prayer requests or break into smaller groups of two to three people to pray for one another. Otherwise, simply close with a simple prayer like the one below:

Dear heavenly Father,

Thank you for giving us your Word. Too often we take it for granted and let it sit on the shelf. Or we pick and choose what we want to believe or want to obey and ignore the difficult portions of Scripture. Forgive us for taking so lightly your words to us. Give us a deep love for your Word, and help us to let it do its work in us of teaching, rebuking, correcting, and training in righteousness. We love you—help us to also love your Word and be people of the Word.

Amen.

Reflect

Before the next group meeting, spend some time reflecting on what you have learned about the Bible.

> *Such things were written in the Scriptures long ago to teach us. And the Scriptures give us hope and encouragement as we wait patiently for God's promises to be fulfilled.*
>
> Romans 15:4

- What is your current relationship with Scripture? Do your habits in the last month support the notion that you believe the Bible is "given by inspiration of God to be the rule of faith and life"? Are you satisfied with the part Scripture plays in your life, both in terms of time spent in the Word and your obedience to it? Journal about where you are and where you'd like to be with regard to being a person of the Word.

- Do you still have questions about the reliability of Scripture? What are some further steps you could take to research and learn more about it?

- What are some habits and practices you will implement this week to help you love and obey God's Word? How can you foster a greater love for the Bible in others? Here are some ideas to get you started: Write out Scripture passages. Study the Bible with others. Use art to help deepen your experience of God's Word. Listen to sermons or expository teaching of Scripture.

Prepare

Session 5 covers chapters 10 and 11, "Hell on Earth?" and "Cosmic Child Abuse?" Read those chapters in preparation for your next meeting. As you read, think about these questions:

- Why would a loving God permit his people to suffer?

- How is judgment consistent with God's love and mercy?

How Do Christians Answer the Tough Questions?

The idea of fire and brimstone, of a burning lake of sulfur where some people will spend eternity, is not popular. Maybe it never has been—surely people of all times prefer not to think about such awful things as judgment and hell—but in this day and age it's especially unpopular. What Christians took for granted a few decades ago is now up for debate, and those who hold to a literal hell often feel like they're losing the debate.

But the Bible holds firmly to the idea that there is a judgment, and after that there is a separation between those who are saved and those who are not. Those who have not trusted in Jesus for their salvation go to a place called hell, forever cut off from God's love and goodness.

That's why Jesus died. If you take away the doctrines of sin, judgment, hell, and atonement, you also take away the need for the Cross. Sin isn't a big problem if it doesn't bring with it big consequences. But it does have big consequences—separation from God's love unless you are reconciled to him and adopted into his family. And one day (either at our death or Jesus' second coming—whichever comes first) that opportunity will be closed to us.

This is what makes the gospel so beautiful. God is willing and able to deal with sin on our behalf, since he knows we can't resolve it ourselves. The cross of Christ wouldn't be glorious if we didn't need it. And heaven wouldn't be such a wonderful destination if there weren't a place to quarantine evil so it can no longer affect us. These doctrines are essential to the Christian faith and are what give us true hope.

Leader's Note

Up to this point we've been talking about topics that group participants might be able to stay detached from. This week everything hits home. You can't talk about these doctrines—judgment, hell, sin, the Atonement, and suffering—without hitting a nerve. And that's a good thing; we need to grapple with the painful parts of life in order to have a robust foundation for our faith. Your goal this week is to navigate these difficult issues with a spirit of gentleness while standing firm in the truth.

> *Every time we turn from the truth of God, we introduce hell into the world. Every time we call evil "good" and good "evil," we create little pockets of hell on earth. But that's not the whole story. The Bible teaches that hell is also an actual place.*
>
> *Another Gospel?*, page 183

Read

Chapters 10 and 11 ("Hell on Earth?" and "Cosmic Child Abuse?") in *Another Gospel?*

Watch Video Session 5

In this session, Alisa invites J. Warner Wallace back to discuss tough questions about biblical justice, the goodness of God, and heaven and hell. Jot down a few notes to help you remember what you heard.

- How have you thought about the tough questions of the faith that Christians have wrestled with for centuries?

- Why does believing in a good and holy God require judgment and a literal hell?

- Why is the death of Jesus on the cross so crucial to our understanding of God and ourselves?

As Wesleyan's we are in the middle — Not double — predestinarians

Discuss

Work through the following questions with your group. Make sure to leave enough time to really dig into questions 8 through 13 (those are the ones that include Scripture) and to spend a few minutes in prayer.

1. What was your primary childhood fear? Is that still your greatest fear? If you feel comfortable, share some of the things that keep you up at night with anxiety.

2. What are some of the biblical images of hell? How do these images either support or challenge what you've always believed about hell?

> God's wrath for sin ensures that his followers will not spend eternity coexisting with sin. Through the sacrificial death of Jesus, we are invited into an eternal Kingdom that will vanquish sin and death forever.
>
> *Another Gospel?*, page 188

The Bible clearly teaches that hell is a place of punishment after judgment and that the people who are shut out of the Kingdom of God end up there. Once we've accepted the fact that hell is a literal place, we must next grapple with what that means for Christians.

3. Alisa points out three common misconceptions of hell: that people in hell are repentant (rather, they are in ongoing rebellion), that the devil rules there and enjoys it (rather, God created hell as a place of punishment *for* the devil and fallen angels), and that everyone gets the same punishment (rather, the Bible speaks of sin and judgment in terms of varying degrees of severity). What do these assertions tell

us about the character of God? About the nature of hell?

Imagine an existence completely devoid of anything good. Without any passing feeling of peace or joy. No beauty. No hope. No love. Nothing to look forward to. Utter despair. Forever trapped within the torment of a bad dream. It's difficult for us to imagine such a state because all of us, from the most hardened atheist to the most ardently devoted Christian, have no idea what life would be like outside of the presence of God's goodness and love. We all experience God's presence in the world. This is what theologians refer to as "common grace," and we don't even have a category for what it would be like to be conscious apart from that reality. . . . [Hell is] life apart from the love and goodness of God and under the complete control and domination of sin.

Another Gospel?, page 191

4. Why is it necessary and just for hell to exist?

Hell is not some kind of divine torture chamber in which God sadistically enjoys the torment of those who reject him. It's God giving them their way. Hell is a place for those who reject God. And God will not force anyone into his Kingdom who doesn't want to be under his rule. And he can't let sin and corruption in the door, even for those who want the benefits of heaven but don't want to turn from their sin to follow him.

Another Gospel?, pages 194–195

Once we've got straight in our minds that a holy and just God must deal with sin, we come to the glorious truth that he did so by sending his own Son to pay the penalty we deserved. He provided the cure to our sin sickness and the payment for our sins. But even here, progressive Christians wish to deny the necessity and efficacy of the Cross. This is the heart of our faith, and we must get this part right.

5. How can you make sense of the fact that a flawed Christian—even a convicted murderer—will go to heaven, while a very kind unbeliever who devotes himself to serving others will go to hell?

6. Alisa writes, "An attack on the Cross is an attack on the very core of what it means to be a Christian . . . [and] on the nature of God himself" (page 201). How do progressives characterize the Cross—in their minds, why did Jesus die, and what does his death do for us? How does this differ from the biblical view of the Cross?

The type of wrath and justice that is usually rejected by progressives is not the biblical version, but a straw man based on the type of wrath that humans experience rather than the true wrath of God. . . . The wrath of God is not a divine temper tantrum triggered by erratic feelings of offense and hatred. The wrath of God is not petty or spiteful. It is the controlled and righteous judgment of anything that opposes the Lord's perfect nature and love. . . . The wrath of God means that there will be justice for the victims of the Holocaust.

Another Gospel?, pages 213–215

7. What does the biblical image of God's wrath as a cup teach us about God and judgment? How is God's wrath evidence of his love?

> *Every sin causes damage, and someone pays for the damage every single time.*
>
> *Another Gospel?*, page 217

The cross of Christ is central to all of Scripture. It was first made known in the Garden of Eden that sin causes separation between God and humanity, and that it ultimately leads to death. But God promised to send a deliverer (Genesis 3:15). In Exodus the blood of a lamb marked God's people and they were saved. In Leviticus we learn about the need for a blood sacrifice to atone for sin. In the Prophets we learn that the Messiah would suffer as he saved God's people. Finally Jesus came, and his death and resurrection made a way for humankind to be reconciled to God, declared righteous, and live free from the curse of sin and death. The Cross is on every page of God's Word.

Read Hebrews 2:14-18:

> Because God's children are human beings—made of flesh and blood—the Son also became flesh and blood. For only as a human being could he die, and only by dying could he break the power of the devil, who had the power of death. Only in this way could he set free all who have lived their lives as slaves to the fear of dying.
>
> We also know that the Son did not come to help angels; he came to help the descendants of Abraham. Therefore, it was necessary for him to be made in every

respect like us, his brothers and sisters, so that he could
be our merciful and faithful High Priest before God.
Then he could offer a sacrifice that would take away the
sins of the people. Since he himself has gone through
suffering and testing, he is able to help us when we are
being tested.

8. What words and phrases in this passage emphasize the
   necessity of the Cross?

9. What theological doctrines does this passage present?
   Parse out everything you can find about sin, salvation,
   and the work of Christ.

10. How might this passage offer comfort and challenge
    to those who wonder if the Cross was unnecessary or
    evidence that God is a cosmic child abuser?

> *Those who denounce God's wrath or accuse the biblical God of being a moral monster are often the very same people who complain that he allows suffering and evil in the world. Yet Scripture tells us of a God who not only gives us an answer for the problem of evil but literally becomes the answer. God looked on the evil and sin of the world, stepped into his own creation, and took our sins upon himself to effectively end sin and evil forever.*
>
> *Another Gospel?*, page 219

Read John 10:11-18:

I am the good shepherd. The good shepherd sacrifices his life for the sheep. A hired hand will run when he sees a wolf coming. He will abandon the sheep because they don't belong to him and he isn't their shepherd. And so the wolf attacks them and scatters the flock. The hired hand runs away because he's working only for the money and doesn't really care about the sheep.

I am the good shepherd; I know my own sheep, and they know me, just as my Father knows me and I know the Father. So I sacrifice my life for the sheep. I have other sheep, too, that are not in this sheepfold. I must bring them also. They will listen to my voice, and there will be one flock with one shepherd.

The Father loves me because I sacrifice my life so I may take it back again. No one can take my life from me. I sacrifice it voluntarily. For I have the authority to lay it down when I want to and also to take it up again. For this is what my Father has commanded.

11. What does this passage teach about Jesus' death on the cross? List all the truths you can find here about the who, what, how, and why of the Cross. How does this passage refute the progressives' arguments or misconceptions (see question 6)?

12. What threats do the sheep in this passage face? What protections and pleasures do they experience?

13. What do you learn about God in this passage—what is he like? How does that image compare with the straw man God that progressives are so troubled by?

Pray

Close your time together in prayer. If time allows, take prayer requests, or break into smaller groups of two to three people to pray for one another. Otherwise, simply close with a simple prayer like the one below:

Dear heavenly Father,

These are hard but glorious truths. You are perfectly just and merciful. We are so thankful that you are holy, but we also know that same holiness requires that the law be fulfilled, and we can't do that on our own. Yet you have made a way; you took upon yourself the punishment we deserved so that we can be free of sin and death forever. As we grapple with the pain of this world and our heartache over those who reject you, keep reminding us of your great mercy and love that have made a way for us to be with you forever. Thank you for your glorious, unending grace.

Amen.

> *A robust theology of the Cross is what will withstand the storms, sufferings, persecutions, and hardships that Jesus promised would confront those who are his true followers.*
>
> *Another Gospel?, page 216*

Reflect

Before the next group meeting, spend some time reflecting on what you have learned about judgment, hell, and the atonement.

- Are these theological doctrines new to you? What new insights did you gain from studying and discussing them this week?

- Are there questions you still have about these important truths? What are some further steps you could take to research and learn about these doctrines?

- Spend some time meditating on Isaiah 53. Jesus suffered for you, and it was the perfect, all-sufficient sacrifice that saves you for all eternity.

Prepare

Session 6 is our wrap-up, covering chapter 12, "Reconstruction," in *Another Gospel?* As you read the final chapter in preparation for your next meeting, think about these questions:

- How has your understanding of the Christian faith and its key doctrines grown in the past several weeks?

- In light of everything you've read and discussed, what is going to be different about the way you approach your walk with the Lord?

Session 6

How Shall We Live?

Stories of "deconstructed" faith fill our news feeds as pastors and teachers walk away from historic Christianity. Sometimes the deconstruction hits closer to home—friends and family members may be losing the faith we once shared with them. It's difficult to talk to them when we are so heartbroken by the lies they've bought into. We marvel that people we learned with and worshiped alongside for so many years could be so blinded to the truth. Our conversations with them are awkward and stilted, and we feel like we can't win the arguments they start with us. We never thought we'd end up in a place where believing and standing up for the Bible makes us feel alone.

Or maybe it's *your* faith that is in deconstruction. Some of the arguments made by progressive Christians sound reasonable to you, and you're not sure exactly what you believe. Or perhaps the church you've attended for many years has taken a turn that has left you disoriented. "For the Bible tells me so" now sounds immature and cliché. If that's where you are, this week is your opportunity to summarize everything you've been learning and make some decisions about where you're going to go next.

Deconstructed faith doesn't have to be the end of the story. What was torn down can be rebuilt, stronger than ever. The story of the wise man who built his house on the rock can be your story—and the story of your loved ones who seem to be leaving the faith—even if it means abandoning the mansion you built on the sand. Storms are a normal part of life, and at times the weak parts of our belief systems will be damaged. The question is, how are we going to rebuild? Will we turn back to the Rock of Ages and ask him what's true? Will we shore up the foundation so we can be stronger than ever? Or will we keep pulling at the ruins of our faith and let the splintered wood and debris remain? The choice is ours—reconstruct so we can stand firm in the truth or let ourselves be blown around by every wind of culture or circumstance until eventually nothing remains of the faith we once held dear.

This final session is a chance to look back at what we've studied and reflected on over the past several weeks, and then look forward to what you are going to do about it. What is the foundation of the Christian faith, and how can you rebuild something stronger than what you started with so you are ready to face the storms of life? Don't let the story end here. Keep on learning, studying, and building a life of faith.

Leader's Note

The reading was a little shorter this week, so hopefully people were able to spend some time grappling with the realities of heaven and hell, grace and judgment, and how those realities fit into our salvation story. Now we're ready to summarize what we've learned over this entire study and reconstruct our faith on the foundation we've been building together.

Some of these questions are similar to questions from previous sessions. That's intentional; the goal here is to review all the ground we've covered so participants can walk away with answers to the questions they've been asking and vocabulary to share their insights with others who ask the same questions.

> *Progressive Christianity offers me nothing of value. It gives no hope for the afterlife and no joy in this one. It offers a hundred denials with nothing concrete to affirm.*
>
> Another Gospel?, page 238

Read

Chapter 12, "Reconstruction," in *Another Gospel?*

Watch Video Session 6

Listen for answers to the following questions, and jot down a few notes to help you remember what you heard.

- What are some benefits of questioning and discarding the false beliefs we may have uncritically picked up from our faith environments?

- How can we help those who are going through a time of questioning, doubt, or faith deconstruction?

- What are the essential beliefs of historic Christianity?

Discuss

Work through the following questions with your group. Be sure to take good notes so you'll have something to refer back to when your friends actually ask you questions (see items 3 through 8).

1. Alisa uses the image of forgetting one piece of a LEGO creation and having to backtrack and rebuild so the structure can stand. What parts of your faith have been rebuilt as a result of this study?

2. What parts of your faith structure still need some shoring up? Where are you still feeling lost, confused, or adrift?

We don't get to completely redefine who God is and how he works in the world and call it Christian.

Another Gospel?, page 239

Believing in the Bible isn't what saves you, but the gospel can only be fully known if the Bible actually is the inerrant and inspired Word of God. The Chicago Statement on Biblical Inerrancy acknowledges that a confession of a belief in inerrancy is not necessary for salvation, but a rejection of it would not come without grave consequences.

Another Gospel?, page 233

We've spent five weeks examining the reasons for doubt and deconstruction that so many Christians are engaging in. Now let's talk about how we can engage in reconstruction. The answers to these questions will help you not only remember everything you've learned, but also practice responding to those who are facing similar faith crises.

3. What are the core doctrines a person must believe in order to be saved?

4. What are some theological doctrines that fall into the "nonessential" category—things that well-meaning Christians can disagree on and still be saved?

5. How would you answer a friend who says that surely a good God would save everyone (universalism)?

> *If you recognize the truth about yourself, you know how desperately you need God (human depravity). If you cry out for him to save you from your sin (Christ's atoning death) and trust him for your salvation (the necessity of faith), all while knowing deep in your gut that you can't save yourself (the necessity of grace), things get real. These are not intellectual mind games. These beautiful truths about reality usher in the salvation of our souls as our fallen hearts are reconciled to God himself! These "propositions" are exciting news to the desperate sinner.*
>
> *Another Gospel?*, page 234

6. How would you answer friends who say they just can't be a part of a church that has so many abuses and problems, or who declare that Christianity is just an outdated religion of oppression by white men?

7. How would you answer a friend who denies the reliability of the Bible or declares that it is just an ancient record of the Christian faith, and who insists that we know better now?

8. How would you answer a friend who says that Christ's death is merely an example for us to follow or, worse, evidence that God is a cosmic child abuser?

We don't get to make the rules and do what is right in our own eyes and yet claim to be followers of Jesus. Our only option is to do it his way or not at all.

Another Gospel?, pages 239–240

When Paul talks about the armor Christians should wear to help them stand firm in the faith, ready to fight the lies of the enemy and the forces of darkness, he starts with the belt of truth (Ephesians 6:14). That's because the battle starts in our mind, with what we think about and know. We need to understand what Jesus has done, what it means for us, and who we are in him. We need to know how those truths anchor us not only to Christ, but also to a new community of believers who are standing alongside us in the battle for truth. We will be ready for action when we have fitted ourselves with the full-orbed gospel truth that counteracts false teaching and provides armor against the enemy. That is how we can stand firm.

But that doesn't mean we won't bear the scars of battle. Alisa writes, "When I walk now, I limp a little. When I read the Bible, I no longer read with innocent eyes not yet clouded by skepticism and doubt. But I'd rather walk with a limp on solid ground than run with strong legs on breaking ice. My song has changed, too, as I have found beauty in the struggle" (page 235). The fight hasn't been easy. It's been worth it and we've grown stronger because of it, but we may walk with a limp for the rest of our lives. In those moments when we feel wounded by the fight, we can run to Jesus. He is the way, the truth, and the life (John 14:6), and in him we have full and unhindered access to our good heavenly Father who loves us and engages with us in all our struggles.

Psalm 46 is a beautiful reminder of where we can find stability in the storms of life. Read it aloud together.

> God is our refuge and strength,
> always ready to help in times of trouble.
> So we will not fear when earthquakes come
> and the mountains crumble into the sea.
> Let the oceans roar and foam.
> Let the mountains tremble as the waters surge!
>
> A river brings joy to the city of our God,
> the sacred home of the Most High.
> God dwells in that city; it cannot be destroyed.
> From the very break of day, God will protect it.
> The nations are in chaos,
> and their kingdoms crumble!
> God's voice thunders,
> and the earth melts!
> The LORD of Heaven's Armies is here among us;
> the God of Israel is our fortress.

Come, see the glorious works of the LORD:
    See how he brings destruction upon the world.
He causes wars to end throughout the earth.
    He breaks the bow and snaps the spear;
    he burns the shields with fire.
"Be still, and know that I am God!
    I will be honored by every nation.
    I will be honored throughout the world."
The LORD of Heaven's Armies is here among us;
    the God of Israel is our fortress.

9. What threats are listed in this psalm? What threats do you face as you build your life on Jesus—what things might eat away at your foundation if it's not strong enough?

10. Where does the psalmist find stability? List the images and names used for God in this passage.

11. How can stillness and quiet help us find strength? How do you find stillness before God in the midst of busyness or doubt?

12. As you leave the group, what are some new insights that you will carry with you?

13. What new actions do you plan to take as a result of the truths you've studied together?

Pray

Close your time together in prayer. You might pray by name for friends and family members who are struggling with these questions and doubts. Include a prayer of dedication, committing yourself and one another to continue your search for truth. You can use the words below or your own.

Dear Jesus,

Thank you for being the way, the truth, and the life. We know that no one can be saved apart from you. Help us learn to worship you with all our heart, soul, mind, and strength and to love others in such a way that they see the truth of the gospel in our lives. Help us to keep on asking, seeking, and knocking after truth—we know that at the end of our search we will find you, the author and perfecter of our faith. And help our loved ones who are struggling in their search for truth. Let them see you for who you are and turn to worship and serve you. May we all one day bow together before your throne, in awe of who you are and all that you have done.

Amen.

While God's grace is free, it does not come cheap.

Another Gospel?, page 237

Reflect

Spend some time reflecting on what you have learned during this study and deciding what you'd like to do with your new knowledge.

- Look again at your Belief Inventory on pages 15–22. Have any of your answers changed since completing the sessions? Which ones? In what way?

- Make a list of propositions about what you believe about yourself, God, and your relationship with God.

I believe I am . . .

I believe God is . . .

I believe Jesus is . . .

I believe the Holy Spirit is . . .

I believe this about the Cross . . .

I believe this about judgment and hell . . .

I believe this about heaven and eternal life . . .

I believe the Bible is . . .

I believe the church is/should . . .

The bottom-line truth that I will build my life on is this:

- What questions has this study raised for you that you'd like to study in more depth? Consult the list of resources on pages 245–250 of *Another Gospel?* or visit alisachilders.com for some suggested resources.

- What next step will you take in building your faith? It might be

  ☐ a spiritual discipline or habit you plan to implement

  ☐ a way you plan to engage with friends or family members who are raising some of the questions discussed in this book

  ☐ some area of learning you want to explore further

  ☐ a step of leadership you know God is challenging you to take

You made it! We hope this study has been challenging and helpful. We hope you have some ideas and answers to core faith issues you didn't have before. Most of all, we hope that the words Paul wrote to the Ephesians have come to fruition in your life:

> Ever since I first heard of your strong faith in the Lord Jesus and your love for God's people everywhere, I have not stopped thanking God for you. I pray for you constantly, asking God, the glorious Father of our Lord Jesus Christ, to give you spiritual wisdom and insight so that you might grow in your knowledge of God. I pray that your hearts will be flooded with light so that you can understand the confident hope he has given to those he called—his holy people who are his rich and glorious inheritance.
>
> I also pray that you will understand the incredible greatness of God's power for us who believe him. This is the same mighty power that raised Christ from the dead and seated him in the place of honor at God's right hand in the heavenly realms. Now he is far above any ruler or authority or power or leader or anything else—not only in this world but also in the world to come. God has put all things under the authority of Christ and has made him head over all things for the benefit of the church. And the church is his body; it is made full and complete by Christ, who fills all things everywhere with himself.
>
> EPHESIANS 1:15-23

Make this your prayer for yourself and other group members you've been journeying with as you walk forward in the truth.

About the Authors

ALISA CHILDERS is the author of *Another Gospel?*, a book in which she describes the years-long journey she took as she wrestled with questions that struck at the core of the Christian faith and found the truth.

Alisa was a member of the award-winning CCM recording group ZOEgirl from 1999 to 2006. She is also a wife, a mom, an author, a blogger, and a speaker. She is a popular speaker at apologetics and Christian worldview conferences, women's conferences, and churches. She has been published at The Gospel Coalition, Crosswalk, the Stream, For Every Mom, *Decision* magazine, and the Christian Post. Her blog post "Girl, Wash Your Face? What Rachel Hollis Gets Right . . . and Wrong" received more than one million views.

You can connect with Alisa online at alisachilders.com.

NANCY TAYLOR has written or contributed to more than a dozen books and Bible products, including *God's Call to a Deeper Life* and *Doodle Devotions for Kids*. Her mission is to create resources that help people know God better, love him more deeply, and serve him wholeheartedly. She and her husband, Jeremy, live in Wheaton, Illinois, with their five children. When she's not writing, editing, or doing mom chores, Nancy enjoys traveling and creating jewelry.

CHECK OUT MORE FROM ALISA CHILDERS!

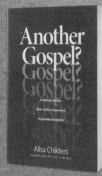

Another Gospel?—In a culture of endless questions, you need solid answers. If you have encountered the ideas of progressive Christianity and aren't sure how to respond, Alisa's journey will show you how to determine—and rest in—what's unmistakably true.

Another Gospel? DVD Experience—In this six-session series, Alisa will teach you how to use discernment, think logically, and make biblically based observations. This DVD experience includes in-depth interviews with *Cold-Case Christianity* author J. Warner Wallace and popular *Waddo You Meme??* YouTube apologist Jon McCray.

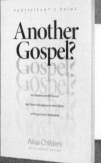

Another Gospel? Participant's Guide—This six-session workbook is designed for use with the companion *Another Gospel? DVD Experience*. This is a great resource for anyone wanting to explore the nuanced topic of progressive Christianity in a group or individually.